THE LITTLE BOOK OF

LIZZO

[unofficial]

First published in Great Britain in 2019 by Hodder & Stoughton
An Hachette UK company
Copyright text © Hodder & Stoughton 2019

1

A CIP catalogue record for this title is available from the British Library.

ISBN 9781529329827

Publisher: Briony Gowlett
Contributing Editor: Grace Paul
Design: Saffron Stocker
Cover illustration: Jade Moore Illustration

Printed and bound by Clays Ltd, Elcograf S.p.A.

Hodder & Stoughton policy is to use papers that are natural, renewable and recyclable products and made from wood grown in sustainable forests. The logging and manufacturing processes are expected to conform to the environmental regulations of the country of origin.

Hodder & Stoughton Ltd
Carmelite House
50 Victoria Embankment
London EC4Y 0DZ
www.hodder.co.uk

THE LITTLE BOOK OF

LIZZO

[unofficial]

QUOTES AND
WISDOM TO
MAKE YOU
FEEL GOOD
AS HELL

HODDER &
STOUGHTON

THE TEN COMMANDMENTS FROM THE CHURCH OF TWERK

Repeat this every day in the morning when you look in the mirror. Embrace your inner positivity.

Thou shalt replace your negative inner voice with Lizzo lyrics

Thou shalt be fuck boy free

Thou shalt love thy body

Thou shalt feel as good as hell every god damn day

Thou shalt love being a bad bitch

Thou shalt not text back, thou shalt tell it straight to their face

Thou art the whole goddamn meal, not the side snack OR thou shalt never ever be the side chick

Thou shalt always fuck it up to the tempo

Thou shalt love yourself and those around you fiercely

Thou shalt be grateful that you exist at the same time as Lizzo

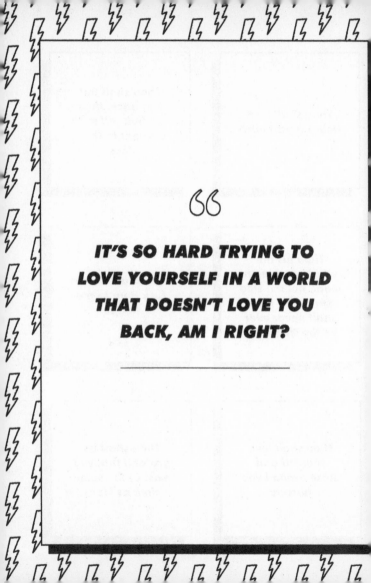

66

IT'S SO HARD TRYING TO LOVE YOURSELF IN A WORLD THAT DOESN'T LOVE YOU BACK, AM I RIGHT?

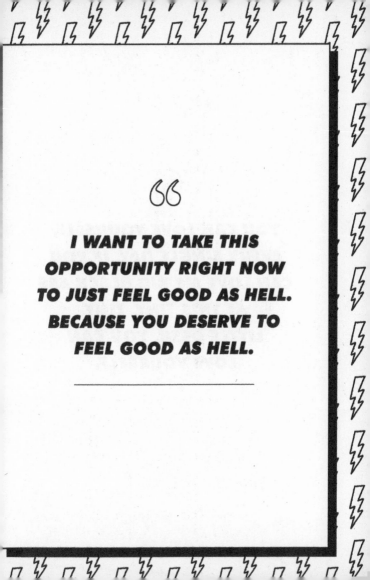

> ## 66
>
> **I WANT TO TAKE THIS OPPORTUNITY RIGHT NOW TO JUST FEEL GOOD AS HELL. BECAUSE YOU DESERVE TO FEEL GOOD AS HELL.**

66

**YOU CAN LOVE YOURSELF.
EVERY SINGLE DAY. IF YOU
CAN LOVE MY BIG BLACK ASS
AT THIS TINY, TINY
LITTLE DESK, YOU CAN
LOVE YOURSELF.**

———————

66

I WANT TO THANK GOD FOR MAKING ME SO JUICY.

66

**I'M DOING THIS FOR MYSELF.
I LOVE CREATING SHAPES
WITH MY BODY, AND I LOVE
NORMALIZING THE DIMPLES
IN MY BUTT OR THE LUMPS
IN MY THIGHS OR MY BACK
FAT OR MY STRETCH MARKS.
I LOVE NORMALIZING MY
BLACK-ASS ELBOWS. I THINK
IT'S BEAUTIFUL.**

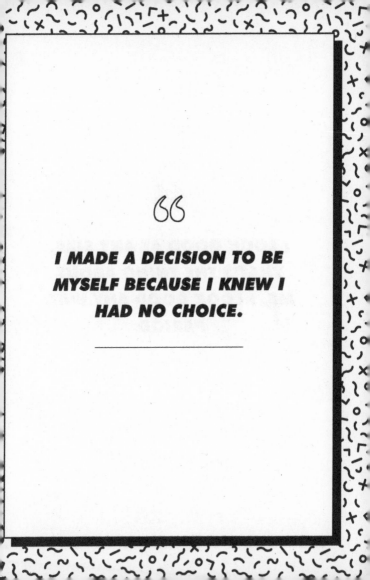

66

I MADE A DECISION TO BE MYSELF BECAUSE I KNEW I HAD NO CHOICE.

66

I LOOK GOOD AT ANY SIZE. THAT'S THE THING ABOUT ME, I LOOK GOOD ANY WAY. PERIOD.

66

I DIDN'T HAVE ENOUGH WOMEN TO LOOK UP TO AND THEY WEREN'T GIVEN ENOUGH SPACE IN THE INDUSTRY TO CARVE OUT A LANE FOR BIG GIRLS THAT ARE BROWN AND BLACK AND WANT TO SING AND DANCE WITHOUT GETTING SHIT TALKED AND BODY SHAMED. I'M OUT HERE AND I SET MY MIND TO IT.

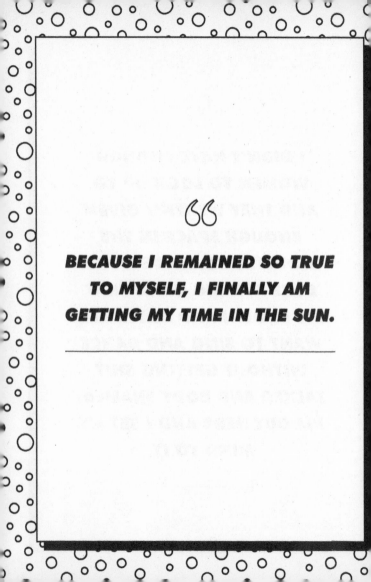

BECAUSE I REMAINED SO TRUE TO MYSELF, I FINALLY AM GETTING MY TIME IN THE SUN.

66

I DON'T THINK THAT LOVING YOURSELF IS A CHOICE. I THINK THAT IT'S A DECISION THAT HAS TO BE MADE FOR SURVIVAL; IT WAS IN MY CASE.

66

I SAY I LOVE MYSELF, AND THEY'RE LIKE, "OH MY GOSH, SHE'S SO BRAVE. SHE'S SO POLITICAL." FOR WHAT? ALL I SAID IS "I LOVE MYSELF, BITCH!"

———

"

EVEN WHEN BODY POSITIVITY IS OVER, IT'S NOT LIKE I'M GOING TO BE A THIN WHITE WOMAN. I'M GOING TO BE BLACK AND FAT. THAT'S JUST HOPPING ON A TREND AND EXPECTING PEOPLE TO BLINDLY LOVE THEMSELVES.

66

THE BODY-POSITIVE MOVEMENT IS THE BODY-POSITIVE MOVEMENT, AND WE HIGH FIVE. WE'RE PARALLEL. BUT MY MOVEMENT IS MY MOVEMENT.

66

**I'M GOING TO STILL BE
TELLING MY LIFE STORY
THROUGH MUSIC. AND IF
THAT'S BODY POSITIVE TO
YOU, AMEN. THAT'S FEMINIST
TO YOU, AMEN. IF THAT'S
PRO-BLACK TO YOU, AMEN.
BECAUSE MA'AM, I'M ALL OF
THOSE THINGS.**

_____

66

BUT I FINALLY REALIZED THAT OWNING UP TO YOUR VULNERABILITIES IS A FORM OF STRENGTH, AND MAKING THE CHOICE TO GO TO THERAPY IS A FORM OF STRENGTH.

66

IT'S UNFAIR FOR US TO ASSUME THAT PEOPLE KNOW HOW TO LOVE THEMSELVES ... [CORPORATIONS HAVE] SPENT DECADES TELLING PEOPLE THEY WEREN'T GOOD ENOUGH AND SELLING THEM AN IDEAL OF BEAUTY.

66

PEOPLE DON'T KNOW HOW TO LOVE THEMSELVES, BECAUSE THEY WERE TRYING TO LOOK LIKE THE MOTHERFUCKER YOU [CORPORATIONS] WERE SELLING THEM!

———————————————

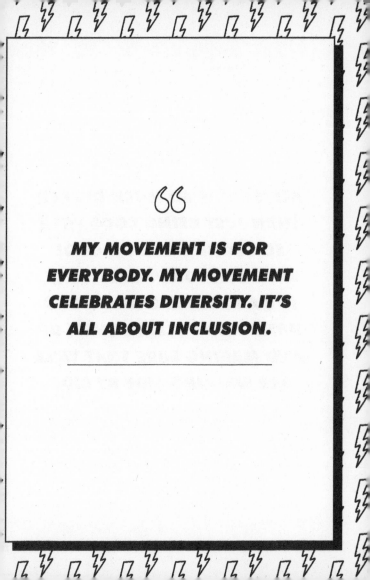

66

MY MOVEMENT IS FOR EVERYBODY. MY MOVEMENT CELEBRATES DIVERSITY. IT'S ALL ABOUT INCLUSION.

66

ALLYSHIP IS SO MUCH DEEPER THAN JUST BEING COOL WITH SOMEONE'S LIFE OR COOL WITH SOMEONE'S EXISTENCE, IT'S ABOUT REACHING OUT A HAND AND PULLING THEM UP AND MAKING SURE THAT YA'LL ARE WALKING SIDE BY SIDE.

66

**I WANT PEOPLE TO REALIZE
THAT FITNESS DOESN'T HAVE A
LOOK OR AN AESTHETIC OR A
WEIGHT. [...] I THINK THAT IT'S
EMPOWERING FOR YOUNG
GIRLS TO SEE THAT IT'S OKAY
TO WORK OUT AND NOT HAVE
A SIX-PACK.**

66

**I DON'T FOLLOW THE
INDUSTRY RULES. I'M JUST
THROWING IT OUT THERE.**

66

*WHEN I HAVE TO MAKE
DECISIONS, I ALWAYS CHOOSE
HONESTY AND I ALWAYS STAY
TRUE TO MYSELF, BECAUSE I
KNOW AT THE END OF THE
DAY THAT IS WHAT'S GOING
TO REMAIN. THAT IS WHAT'S
GOING TO BE THE LEGEND:
THAT I WAS TRUE TO MYSELF
AND THAT I HONORED
EVERY PERSON BY STAYING
TRUTHFUL TO THEM.*

_____

66

I WANT YOU TO GO HOME TONIGHT, LOOK IN THE MIRROR AND SAY "I LOVE YOU, YOU ARE BEAUTIFUL AND YOU CAN DO ANYTHING!"

66

**I BELIEVE WE CAN SAVE
THE WORLD IF WE SAVE
OURSELVES FIRST. AND YOU
ALL CAN CHANGE THE WORLD!**

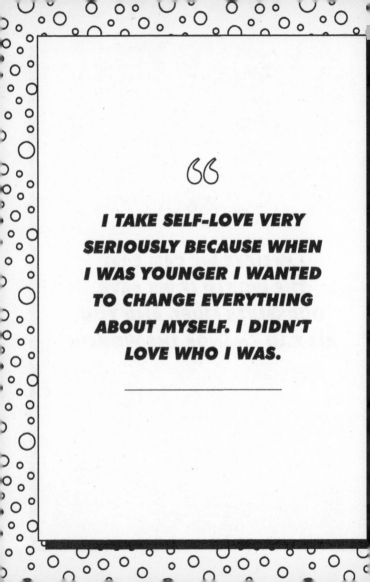

66

**I TAKE SELF-LOVE VERY
SERIOUSLY BECAUSE WHEN
I WAS YOUNGER I WANTED
TO CHANGE EVERYTHING
ABOUT MYSELF. I DIDN'T
LOVE WHO I WAS.**

66

**THE REASON I DIDN'T LOVE
WHO I WAS IS BECAUSE I
WAS TOLD I WASN'T LOVABLE
BY THE MEDIA, BY [PEOPLE
AT] SCHOOL, BY NOT SEEING
MYSELF IN BEAUTY ADS,
BY NOT SEEING MYSELF IN
TELEVISION ... BY LACK OF
REPRESENTATION.**

66

**NOW THE SONG THAT MADE
ME WANT TO QUIT IS THE
SONG THAT EVERYONE'S
FALLING IN LOVE WITH ME
FOR, WHICH IS SUCH
A TESTAMENT TO JOURNEYS:
YOUR DARKEST DAY TURNS
INTO YOUR BRIGHTEST
TRIUMPH.**

66

**I HAD EVERYTHING ELSE:
THE HARD WORK, THE GOOD
MUSIC, TOURING – BUT THEN
THERE'S THAT EXTRA-SPECIAL
MAGIC THAT NOBODY REALLY
KNOWS WHAT IT IS THAT CAN
REALLY CHANGE YOUR LIFE.**

66

**I LOOK IN THE MIRROR
NOW AND THINK, "DAMN,
I DON'T NEED ANYBODY TO
TELL ME I LOOK GOOD."
I DON'T EVEN NEED THE
FUCKING MIRROR TO.**

66

**I'M NOT WRITING THESE
SONGS TO REMIND MYSELF
ONE DAY THAT I'M THAT
BITCH, I WANT TO <u>BE</u> THAT
BITCH – AND SINGING THEM
EVERY DAY HELPS
ME MANIFEST THAT.**

66

**MY MUSIC IS RELATABLE
BECAUSE EVERYBODY
WANTS TO BE BETTER, LOVE
THEMSELVES, AND BE 100 PER
CENT THAT BITCH.**

66

MY JOB AS AN ARTIST ISN'T MERELY TO SING. MY ROLE IS TO DELIVER SOMETHING THAT HELPS PEOPLE.

———————

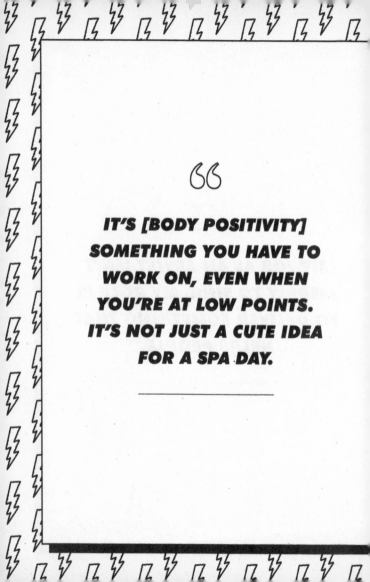

66

IT'S [BODY POSITIVITY] SOMETHING YOU HAVE TO WORK ON, EVEN WHEN YOU'RE AT LOW POINTS. IT'S NOT JUST A CUTE IDEA FOR A SPA DAY.

66

ARE YOU STRAIGHT? DO YOU LIKE BIG GIRLS? [TO KAMERON MICHAELS, RUPAUL'S DRAG RACE, SERIES 10, EPISODE 10]

66

I DON'T WALLOW INTO THE FUTURE OR THE PAST LIKE I DID. I ASK, "WHAT AM I FEELING RIGHT NOW?"

66

THE IMPORTANT THING IS MAKING SURE THIS SHIT DON'T BECOME A TREND. [...] BODY POSITIVITY HAS TO BE MAINSTREAM.

66

**YOU'VE GOT TO ASK AND
YOU'LL RECEIVE.**

"

**WE SHOULD LOOK AT
OUR BODIES AS VEHICLES
FOR SUCCESS, AND NOT A
SIGNIFIER OF WHO YOU ARE,
HOW GOOD YOUR PUSSY IS,
IF DUDES LIKE YOU OR NOT,
OR IF YOU CAN FIT CERTAIN
CLOTHES ... THAT'S NOT WHAT
YOUR BODY'S FOR.**

66

EVERYONE SHOULDN'T HAVE TO HIT ROCK BOTTOM TO LOVE THEMSELVES [...] THAT'S JUST THE SOCIETY WE'RE ALL UNFORTUNATELY BORN IN - THE ONE WHERE YOU HAVE TO HIT YOUR WORST AND HATE YOURSELF IN ORDER TO LOVE YOURSELF. THOSE LAWS ONLY EXIST BECAUSE SELF-HATE IS SO PREVALENT. BODY POSITIVITY ONLY EXISTS BECAUSE BODY NEGATIVITY IS THE NORM.

66

I WOULD SLEEP IN MY CAR AND EAT CARDBOARD BEFORE I SOLD HER. [TALKING ABOUT SASHA FLUTE]

———————

66

**DON'T ASK ME WHAT
THEY WANT YOU TO ASK ME,
ASK ME WHAT YOU WANT
TO ASK ME. ASK ME ABOUT
MY VIBRATORS.**

———————————

"

SO, AT FIRST, I LIKE TO REACH OUT AND LET PEOPLE KNOW HOW I'M FEELING. I'M LIKE, "YO, I'M NOT FEELING GOOD TODAY. I'M NOT WITH IT." COMMUNICATING IS SO HARD TO DO, BUT ONCE YOU LEARN HOW TO DO IT, IT CHANGES EVERYTHING.

"

**I DON'T REALLY HAVE
NOTHING SERIOUS I WOULD
SAY TO 25-YEAR-OLD ME.
IT WASN'T THAT LONG AGO,
I'M KIND OF THE SAME BITCH,
EXCEPT I JUST HAVE
BETTER HAIR.**

66

I WANT TO FEEL GOOD.

_____

"

**I NEED THIS MUSIC TO
BE MY THERAPY BECAUSE
I HAVE BEEN SOLO AND I
REFUSE TO LIVE LIFE LIKE
THAT ANYMORE.**

66

I DEFINITELY DIDN'T HAVE, GROWING UP, A LOT OF PEOPLE TO LOOK UP TO WHO LOOKED LIKE ME WHO WERE CALLED BEAUTIFUL.

66

I REALIZED NO MATTER HOW I LOOK, SOMEONE'S ALWAYS GONNA HAVE SOMETHING TO SAY ABOUT IT. BUT ALL THAT MATTERS IS WHAT I THINK.

66

**WHEN PEOPLE LOOK
AT MY BODY AND BE LIKE,
"OH MY GOD, SHE'S SO
BRAVE," IT'S LIKE, "NO I'M
NOT. I'M JUST FINE. I'M JUST
ME. I'M JUST SEXY."**

———————————

66

I DON'T LIKE IT WHEN PEOPLE THINK IT'S HARD FOR ME TO SEE MYSELF AS BEAUTIFUL.

66

**DON'T SHRINK YOURSELF
AROUND OTHER PEOPLE
BECAUSE YOU BELIEVE THAT
THEIR STAR SHINES BRIGHTER
THAN YOURS.**

66

I AM CELEBRATING MY INDIVIDUALITY; AND THE THINGS THAT MAKE ME AN INDIVIDUAL ARE WHAT I DO, IT IS MY SKIN COLOR, IT IS MY HAIR. YOU CAN CELEBRATE YOUR INDIVIDUALITY AS WELL.

66

IF MY ENERGY CAN'T SURVIVE IN THE ROOM THEN ... I DON'T KNOW WHAT'S WRONG WITH THAT ROOM, BUT THAT ROOM NEEDS JESUS!

66

I HEAR A WOMAN WHO'S LIKE, "OH MY GOD, I CAN LOVE MYSELF, SO WHY IS IT SO HARD TO BE LOVED BY SOMEONE ELSE? I LOVE MYSELF, HOW COME YOU CAN'T LOVE ME?" I THINK THAT SHE'S TRYING TO GRAPPLE WITH THAT HARSH REALITY. IT'S LIKE, NO MATTER HOW MUCH YOU LOVE YOURSELF YOU CAN'T MAKE SOMEONE LOVE YOU.

66

ONE DAY I WAS LIKE "YO, I'M GOING TO BE IN THIS BODY FOREVER, I'M GOING TO BE THIS BITCH FOREVER SO IT'S EITHER LIKE YOU LIVE YOUR LIFE NOT LIKING HER OR YOU LIVE YOUR LIFE TRYING TO LOVE HER." SO EVER SINCE THEN I'VE BEEN WORKING ON LOVING MYSELF.

66

**AS A GROWN-ASS WOMAN,
I WORK REALLY HARD ON
SELF-CARE, ON SELF-LOVE
AND TRYING TO BE POSITIVE
AND IT SHOWS.**

66

THE PART THAT MAKES ME SAD IS THAT I WANT OTHER PEOPLE WHO LOOK LIKE ME TO HAVE OPPORTUNITIES, TO BE SEEN AND TO GET JOBS. AND I DON'T KNOW IF IT IS WORKING OR NOT BECAUSE I AM SO IN THE MIDDLE OF IT, BUT I WILL SAY THAT I AM DOING EVERYTHING I CAN. I AM TRYING.

66

**I LOVE MY BODY. NO MATTER
WHAT ANGLE YOU SHOOT IT
AT, NO MATTER THE LIGHTING,
MY BODY IS JUST SO FUCKING
BEAUTIFUL ALL THE TIME.
I MAY TALK SHIT ABOUT IT
SOMETIMES, BUT FUCK. SHE'S
STILL A BAD BITCH.**

66

**THE TERM "BODY POSITIVE" ...
TECHNICALLY, IT ONLY EXISTS
BECAUSE OF BODY SHAMING.**

66

I'M REALLY LEARNING ABOUT HOW TO BE VULNERABLE, BUT ALSO NOT DEFENSELESS.

66

*I HAD TO SHOW MY
BELLY A LOT OF ATTENTION,
A LOT OF LOVE.*

66

I HAVE TO FAKE IT UNTIL I MAKE IT. YOU JUST HAVE TO GAS YOURSELF UP. IT TAKES A LOT OF WORK.

66

**THE FIRST TIME I
PARTICIPATED IN ACTIVISM?
[SIGH] MY WHOLE
BLACK-ASS LIFE.**

66

**I'M ONLY MAKING
POSITIVE MUSIC FROM NOW
ON AND IF ANYBODY THINKS
I'M TOO HAPPY THEN THERE'S
SOMETHING WRONG
WITH YOU.**

66

ONCE YOU ARE FULL OF YOURSELF AND YOU'RE FULL OF THE SELF-LOVE THAT YOU HAVE AND YOU'RE NOT SEARCHING FOR THAT ANYWHERE ELSE, EVERYTHING THAT'S YOURS WILL BE ATTRACTED TO YOU.

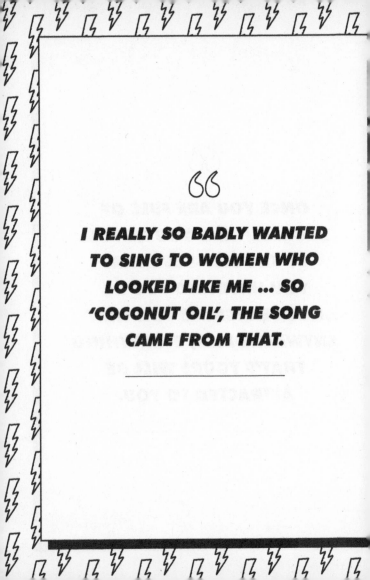

> 66
>
> **I REALLY SO BADLY WANTED TO SING TO WOMEN WHO LOOKED LIKE ME ... SO 'COCONUT OIL', THE SONG CAME FROM THAT.**

66

**IF YOU DON'T TAKE THE
TIME TO GET EVERYTHING,
ALL YOUR BASES COVERED,
ALL YOUR AREAS COVERED,
YOU'RE GOING TO BE DRY
IN SOME AREAS, YOU'RE
GOING TO BE THIRSTY IN
SOME AREAS, YOU'RE NOT
GOING TO BE FULFILLED
IN SOME AREAS. [ON
HOW MOISTURIZING IS A
METAPHOR FOR LIFE]**

"

**THERE'S NOTHING SEXIER
THAN WHEN YOU'RE DANCING
AND WHEN YOU'RE HAPPY,
NOT WHEN YOU'RE TRYING TO
DANCE BUT DANCING.**

66

SO EVERY TIME I RAP
ABOUT BEING A BIG GIRL
IN A SMALL WORLD IT'S
DOING A COUPLE THINGS:
IT'S EMPOWERING MY SELF-
AWARENESS, MY BODY IMAGE,
AND IT'S ALSO MAKING THE
STATEMENT THAT WE ARE ALL
BIGGER THAN THIS, WE'RE A
PART OF SOMETHING BIGGER
THAN THIS, AND WE SHOULD
LIVE IN EACH MOMENT
KNOWING THAT.

66

**I AM A WOMAN, I TREAT
MYSELF WITH RESPECT AND
I LOVE MYSELF, AND I THINK
THAT IF I'M HOLDING MYSELF
TO A CERTAIN ESTEEM AND
KEEPING IT REAL WITH
MYSELF, THEN THAT'S GOING
TO TRANSLATE TO
PEOPLE LIKE ME.**

66

GOING ON THAT JOURNEY OF BEING VULNERABLE WITH SOMEONE WHO I DIDN'T KNOW, AND THEN LEARNING HOW TO BE VULNERABLE WITH PEOPLE THAT I DO KNOW, GAVE ME THE COURAGE TO BE VULNERABLE AS A VOCALIST.

66

**AS AN ARTIST,
WE'RE SUPPOSED TO BE
EMOTING OUR FEELINGS AND
TURNING IT INTO ART THAT IS
TO BE APPRECIATED OR USED
FOR HEALING.**

66

[FEMINISM] IS ABOUT
FAIRNESS BETWEEN MEN AND
WOMEN. I THINK WHAT'S
FAIR IS EQUAL PAY. WHAT'S
FAIR IS GETTING RID OF RAPE
CULTURE AND MISOGYNY.

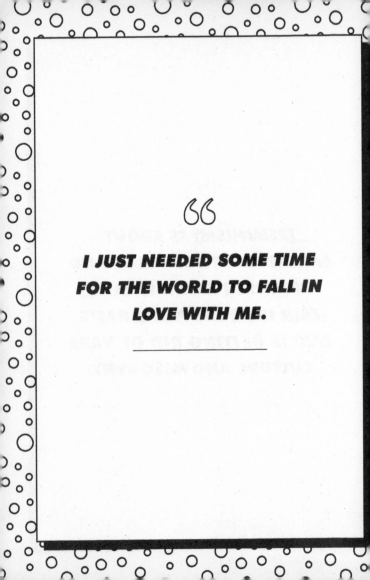

66

**I JUST NEEDED SOME TIME
FOR THE WORLD TO FALL IN
LOVE WITH ME.**

66

**WHEN WE WALK ON THAT
STAGE, WE PUT A SMILE
ON SOMEBODY'S FACE AND
ESPECIALLY OUR OWN FACES.**

66

**I THINK THAT IT'S
SO INTERESTING THAT
BODY POSITIVITY IS NOW
THIS BUZZING TERM.
THERE'S NO TERM FOR BODY
NEGATIVITY BECAUSE IT'S THE
NORM WE EXPECT.**

66

IF I'M HAPPY ON THE INSIDE, THEN EVERYONE'S GONNA FEEL THAT JOY THAT I HAVE FROM THE INSIDE.

66

I NOTICED THAT WHEN I STARTED TO SELF-LOVE AND I STARTED TO SELF-CARE, THE PEOPLE AROUND ME CHANGED. AND THE PEOPLE WHO WERE TOXIC AND NOT GOOD FOR ME, THEY JUST SEGUED OUT.

66

IF I FEEL WORTHY AND WANTED, THEN EVERYBODY GONNA WANT TO EAT MY PUSSY.

———————

66

IF I LOSE SIGHT OF MYSELF FOR A MINUTE, AND I FORGET ME, I'LL BE DOING SOME DUMB SHIT, BRO.

66

**I HAVE A VERY POWERFUL
MOUTH AND I HAVE VERY
POWERFUL WORDS, SO WHEN
I SAY CERTAIN THINGS, I MAKE
SURE I MEAN IT.**

66

**MY SELF-CARE NEEDS TO
CATCH UP WITH MY LIFE.**

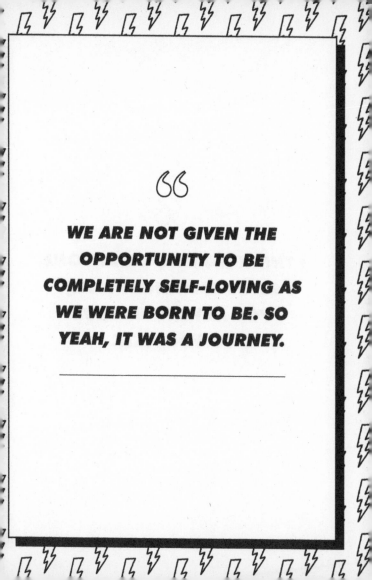

66

WE ARE NOT GIVEN THE OPPORTUNITY TO BE COMPLETELY SELF-LOVING AS WE WERE BORN TO BE. SO YEAH, IT WAS A JOURNEY.

66

I THINK WOMEN, OR ANYONE,
ESPECIALLY RIGHT NOW,
YOU HAVE TO BE TRUE
TO YOURSELF.

———

"

BEING AN INDIVIDUAL WILL GET YOU THERE [TO SUCCESS]. IT'S NOT THE QUICK WAY, IT TAKES A WHILE BUT IT FEELS BETTER IN THE END.

———————————

LIZZBIAN MANIFESTATIONS

Your body is like a cactus, prickly on the outside because you're a bad bitch but, on the inside, you're as soft as butter and you need to take care of her every single day. First of all, manifest your best life like our queen Lizzo does:

Set your intention

Visualize your intention: what does it feel like? What does it look like? What does it taste like? Throw it out to the universe.

Write it down and think about it when you're dancing in front of the mirror every morning.

Believe in the power of your words to give them power.

Surrender to the universe.

Work hard and be grateful.

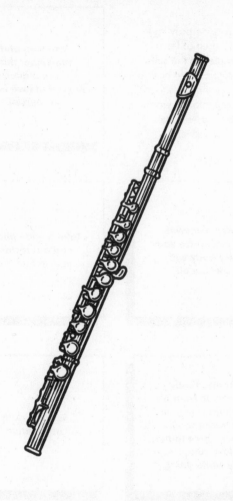

Now, carry on praying to the Church of Lizzo by completing the self-care tasks below to ensure you're putting positive energy out into the world. Have a great day Lizzo style!

Wake up and remember that you're a queen. Bring that love back to yourself

Have a shower and moisturize your juicy body with coconut oil

Take a nude photo and appreciate yourself naked

Dance, really dance, in front of the mirror to your favorite song. Repeat three things you love about your body while doing it

Set your daily affirmation

*Eat food which
nourishes you*

*Remember your
breath is your friend*

*Do not engage with
any fuck boys*

*Communicate
your feelings*

*List three things
you're grateful
for at the end of
the day*

*Go to sleep knowing
that you are enough*

SOURCES

2019 Video Music Awards, 26 August 2019 – pp 6,7

NPR Music Tiny Desk Concert, 29 July 2019 – pp 8,9

Essence, 15 May 2019 – pp 10, 11

Breakfast Club Power, 24 May 2019 – pp 12, 58, 59

Vogue, 1 May 2019 – pp 13, 14

NBC News, 19 April 2019 – pp 15, 20

The Cut, 3 February 2019 – pp 16, 17

Allure , 6 March 2019 – pp 18, 19

Guardian, 19 October 2018 – pp 21, 22

Junkee, 18 April 2019 – pp 23, 24

Billboard, 6 June 2018 – pp 25, 26

Rolling Stone, 19 April 2019 – pp 27, 66, 74

Glastonbury Festival, 29 June 2019 – pp 28, 29

Elle Magazine, 5 September 2019 – pp 30, 31

People Magazine, 24 July 2019 – pp 32, 33

Dazed Magazine, 23 April 2019 – pp 34, 35, 36

Evening Standard, 17 May 2019 – pp 37, 38

RuPaul's Drag Race, Series 10, Episode 10 – pp 39

Playboy, 18 March 2019 – pp 40, 41

Teen Vogue, 15 June 2018 – pp 42, 43, 44

Kexp, 31 July 2019 – pp 45

Marie Claire, 30 July 2019 – pp 46, 47

ET Online, 27 August 2019 – pp 48, 49

I Weigh: In Conversation with Lizzo, 5 April 2019 – pp 50, 51

Glamour Magazine, 28 August 2019 – pp 52, 53

Nylon, 4 September 2019 – pp 54, 55

Clash, 10 May 2019 – pp 56, 57

V Magazine, 29 April 2019 – pp 60, 61

Q on CBC, 22 December 2016 – pp 62

GQ Magazine, 19 April 2019 – pp 63

New York Times, 18 September 2018 – pp 64, 65

The Current, 7 May 2019 – pp 67, 68

Sway's Universe, 16 June 2017 – pp 69, 70, 71

Interview Magazine, 15 September 2014 – pp 72, 73

Vibe, 18 August 2016 – pp 75, 76

Today, 23 August 2019 – pp 77, 78

The Daily Show, 11 April 2019 – pp 79

Quoted By ... With Hoda, 4 June 2019 – pp 80, 81

NME, 31 August 2018 – pp 82, 83, 84

Stylist, 4 September – pp 85, 86

Love Magazine, 30 July 2019 – pp 87, 88